PUBLISHED BY CREATIVE EDUCATION AND CREATIVE PAPERBACKS
P.O. BOX 227, MANKATO, MINNESOTA 56002
CREATIVE EDUCATION AND CREATIVE PAPERBACKS
ARE IMPRINTS OF THE CREATIVE COMPANY
WWW.THECREATIVECOMPANY.US

DESIGN AND PRODUCTION BY CHRISTINE VANDERBEEK
ART DIRECTION BY RITA MARSHALL
PRINTED IN THE UNITED STATES OF AMERICA

PHOTOGRAPHS BY ALAMY (CULTURA CREATIVE, DESIGN PICS INC, NEIL
MCNICOLL), CORBIS (LIESEL BOCKL/MINT IMAGES, BILL FRYMIRE/MASTERFILE,
MARC VAUGHN/MASTERFILE), ISTOCKPHOTO (BRAUNS, DEEPBLUE4YOU, LISE
GAGNE, GIVAGA, HELLEM, JMICHL, LAWRENCESAWYER, MEHMETTORLAK,
MOLOKO88, WITOLDKR1, WORAPUT, WWING), SHUTTERSTOCK (MIKELEDRAY,
PHOTOSYNC, KEITH PUBLICOVER, RIMOM, STEVENRUSSELLSMITHPHOTOS, VOVAN)

LIBRARY OF CONGRESS CATALOGING-IN-PUBLICATION DATA
ROSEN, MICHAEL J.
FISHING GEAR / MICHAEL J. ROSEN.
P. CM. — (REEL TIME)
INCLUDES INDEX.
SUMMARY: A PRIMER ON THE BASIC DOS AND DON'TS OF FISHING, INCLUDING TIPS
ON CHOOSING A PROPER ROD AND REEL, ADVICE ON HOW TO LAND A CATCH, AND
INSTRUCTIONS FOR MAKING A LANDING NET.

ISBN 978-1-60818-773-7 (HARDCOVER)
ISBN 978-1-62832-381-8 (PBK)
ISBN 978-1-56660-815-2 (EBOOK)
THIS TITLE HAS BEEN SUBMITTED FOR CIP PROCESSING UNDER LCCN 2016010296.

CCSS: RI.3.1, 2, 3, 4, 5, 7, 8, 10; RI.4.1, 2, 3, 4, 7, 10; RI.5.1, 2, 4, 10;
RF.3.3, 4; RF.4.3, 4; RF.5.3, 4

FIRST EDITION HC 9 8 7 6 5 4 3 2 1
FIRST EDITION PBK 9 8 7 6 5 4 3 2 1

FISHING GEAR

→ MICHAEL J. ROSEN ←

CREATIVE EDUCATION ⚓ CREATIVE PAPERBACKS

FISHING GEAR → CHAPTER 1

A REEL GOOD TIME

Whether this is your first time fishing or you're an old pro, each outing is unique. The water is different. The weather changes. The fish have grown older—and smarter. Every time you cast your line is different. But the fun and the challenge are always there. So let's get you geared up and ready to fish!

Start by getting a rod and reel. Most sporting goods stores have a selection of sets for younger anglers. Find a rod that feels good in your hand. Try one that is five or six feet (1.5–1.8 m) long. Test the rod. Hold its handle and shake it around. The rod shouldn't bend too much—only at the tip. Try several rods. If it's a tie between two rods, pick the color, shape, and design you like best. Buy the best rod you can. Better materials and finer workmanship make for a quality rod. It's less likely to break, splinter, rust, or lose parts.

You have two choices for reels. The first is a closed-face spinning reel. It is trouble-free, inexpensive, and easy to use. The line is sealed inside a case on top of the rod. A button, worked by your thumb, releases the line. Your other option is the open-face spinning reel. It has no cover or button. The spool hangs under the rod. The bail, a curved bar, controls the line leaving and entering the reel.

reel handle

spool

bail

CLOSED-FACE SPINNING REEL

OPEN-FACE SPINNING REEL

CASTING ABOUT

Fly fishing requires special line and lots of casting practice.

Ready to practice casting? Check that the reel is tightly secured on the rod. The line should be threaded through the guides (the metal rings on the rod) without tangling or circling the rod. Tie a sinker to the end of the line. Leave about six inches (15.2 cm) of line hanging from the rod's tip. Reel in any extra line.

Now find a wide-open area. Pick a target to cast toward. Hold the rod in your dominant hand. Point the tip of the rod just above your target. Push and hold down the reel's button with your thumb. (Or, if you are using an open-face reel, swing the bail over and hold the line with your thumb.)

Casting can be a tricky skill to perfect, but it is important to practice.

Bend your elbow and raise your arm until the tip of the rod just passes your ear and points behind you.

Flick the rod forward and release your thumb at the same time. Start the motion with your wrist. Follow with your forearm until the rod is pointing straight ahead—not quite parallel to the ground. The sinker should send the line out in front of you. Good job! You just did an overhand cast.

What if the line hit the ground right in front of you? Oops! You released your thumb too late. Try again!

Or did the line fly into the air above you? Oops! You released your thumb too soon. Try again!

Practice until you can land the sinker right where you want it. Pick out a target spot. Try to land your line behind, in front of, and to either side of it.

If you are fishing below overhanging trees, use the sidearm cast. Swing your arm to the side rather than over your head. It's the same motion as an overhand cast, but with your arm at a right angle and parallel to the ground.

As you cast your line, keep your eye on your target spot.

DO I HAVE A BITE?

Large fish, such as sockeye salmon, can be challenging to reel in as they fight to get free.

The jiggle and dip of your bobber isn't the only sign of a fish biting. Watch the tip of your rod. It will usually be straight, bending only slightly as the current tugs the line. If it bends down suddenly, that usually means a fish is biting!

Many anglers lightly place one finger on the line in front of the reel. It helps them feel the line's movements. This is useful with smaller fish whose bites make weaker signals. You'll learn to feel the difference between a nibble and a sudden, stronger bite.

Sometimes those "bites" are just your line, and not a fish, that's caught. What can you do? Try to work the snag free.

Pull the rod in one direction and then the other. If you're on shore, walk your line along the bank. Try pulling the hook from the opposite direction. If the end of your line is close, use a long stick or your net to pry at the snag.

Sometimes all you can do is cut your line free, giving up your tackle. This happens to even the most careful angler. If you know you're fishing near a weedy, rocky bottom, bait your hook in a "weedless" way: Bury the point in the bait. Then your hook is less likely to get caught.

Many fish hide from predators—including humans—among weeds, fallen trees, and rocks.

LANDING GEAR

Never pull a fish out of the water without using a net—the hook could tear through the fish's lip.

 net makes landing a fish easier. Never jerk your catch out of the water or leave it dangling in the air. This could break your line, lose the fish, and even cause injury.

Hold your rod with one hand. Grab the net with the other. Slide it in front of the fish. As you lift your line, slip the net under the fish. Once the fish is in the net, ask for a hand from another angler. (This part is easier with two people.) Bring the net toward you until the fish is within reach. Set down your line. Carefully remove the hook. If you want to record your catch, measure it and take a picture. Then, gently return the fish to its wet home.

ACTIVITY: MAKE A LANDING NET

MAKE A NET STRONG ENOUGH TO LAND SMALL- AND MEDIUM-SIZED FISH.

MATERIALS

- pliers
- a strong wire hanger
- five feet (1.5 m) of twine
- a sturdy handle (such as a broom handle, tent pole, or dead tree limb)
- a mesh or string sack (such as ones that hold potatoes, grape-fruits, or oranges)

1 Use pliers to straighten the hanger. Then bend the wire to form a loop. Be careful of the ends! Seek an adult's help, if needed.

2 Repeatedly wrap and knot the twine around one end of the wire and your handle.

3 Thread the free end of the wire through the opening of the sack. Weave the wire in and out of the sack to form the net's rim.

4 Secure the other end of the loop to the handle by repeatedly wrapping and knotting the twine. Now you can use a net the next time you fish!

GLOSSARY

anglers → people who fish

bobber → a small, floating object used to keep the hook at a certain depth

cast → the action used to place a baited line out in the water

current → the direction in which a body of water is moving

sinker → a small weight used to help a baited hook sink

spool → the part of the reel that the line is wound around

tackle → gear used in fishing, such as hooks, sinkers, bobbers, and bait

READ MORE

Bourne, Wade. *The Pocket Fishing Basics Guide: Freshwater Basics, Hook, Line & Sinker*. New York: Skyhorse, 2012.

Parker, Steve. *Fish*. New York: DK, 2005.

WEBSITES

Fishing Tips Depot

http://www.fishingtipsdepot.com/

Find fishing tips by species, technique, and type.

Take Me Fishing: How to Fish

http://www.takemefishing.org/how-to-fish/

Learn more about fishing, and find places to fish near you!

Note: Every effort has been made to ensure that the websites listed above are suitable for children, that they have educational value, and that they contain no inappropriate material. However, because of the nature of the Internet, it is impossible to guarantee that these sites will remain active indefinitely or that their contents will not be altered.

INDEX